300 EMAIL MARKETING TIPS

300 EMAIL MARKETING TIPS

CRITICAL ADVICE, STRATEGIES & IDEAS
TO TURN SUBSCRIBERS INTO
BUYERS & GROW
A SIX-FIGURE BUSINESS WITH EMAIL

300 EMAIL MARKETING TIPS:

CRITICAL ADVICE, STRATEGIES & IDEAS TO TURN SUBSCRIBERS INTO BUYERS & GROW A SIX-FIGURE BUSINESS WITH EMAIL

MEERA KOTHAND

WWW.MEERAKOTHAND.COM

COPYRIGHT © 2019

Contents

You can download the Email Jumpstart Pack at
https://meera.email/300
Sign up for the FREE Email Crash Course at
https://meera.email/challenge

THE BIG, BOLD PROMISE

You're not one of those people…

The skeptics…

The ones waiting with bated breath for another report that email will breathe its last …

The ones who claim that email will be completely replaced by messenger marketing, bots, or the next new fad…

If you were, you'd never have given this book a second glance.

But that doesn't mean you're ecstatic about email.

You may even find it a pain…

One more chore on your endless to-do list as an entrepreneur…One more thing with endless contradictory advice…

Not forgetting your own crippling questions.

What should I send my subscribers?

How do I keep up with email on top of existing content demands?

How are people making money from their email list while I'm stuck here with tanking opens, meager clicks, and pathetic engagement?

Email doesn't get the same hype as social media or content marketing. Call it the inferior cousin if you will...

But you can't ignore the results email marketing gets.

Here are some quick stats that show you how effective email is:

For every $1 spent on email marketing, the average return is $44.25.[1] (**Note:** I find this to be pretty accurate in my own case. Do the math and see if you meet these numbers.)

Social media is important, but an email subscriber is more valuable than a social media follower. If you had 1,000 followers, 1,000 organic visitors, and 1,000 email subscribers, and you tried to sell your offer to all of them, you could expect to convert 5.9 followers, 24.9 searchers, and 42.4 subscribers.[2] According to the Data & Marketing Association,[3] when it comes to purchases made as a result of receiving a marketing message, email has the highest conversion rate of 66%.

Beyond the stats, here are some factors to consider:

THE CASE FOR EMAIL

1. Email gives you more than one opportunity to sell

At any one point in time, only a tiny sliver of your audience is ready to buy from you. In his book, *Sticky Branding*,[4] Jeremy Miller calls this the 3% rule. He states that only 3% of the market is actively looking to buy at any point in time. But he mentions that there is a huge opportunity in the lower 90% of the market.

When done right, email lets you capitalize on the mindshare of this 90% of your audience in a nonsleazy way. People aren't always ready to buy the first time you launch an offer. That doesn't mean that they'll never be interested. I have had people who've bought from me when they've been on my list for a single day and others who've bought a whole six months to a year later. The buying process is not always linear or predictable. When you build a consistent relationship with people even when they're not actively looking for your products and services, you become top of mind when they are indeed in the market to buy.

2. You own your email list

When you embrace email marketing, you're not building your community or tribe on someone else's platform (i.e., Facebook, Pinterest, or Instagram). You won't be scrambling whenever these platforms change their algorithms because you have direct access to your audience.

3. There's less competition

You're not a status update that disappears within minutes and gets buried within people's feeds. You are *in* their inbox and email is what people check every day. Based on stats from email marketing company BlueHornet, almost 34% of American consumers say they check their email "throughout the day."[5]

Isn't everybody's inbox filled with tons of emails?

Sure!

But if your subscriber associates your name with a positive emotion or value and you always deliver on your emails, your emails *will* get opened and read. You will know exactly how to do that by the end of this book. You'll also know how to define the almost mystical word *value* and break down what it stands for.

4. Email helps establish trust

At any time, there are one of six people interacting with your brand: Stranger – Reader – Subscriber – Engaged Subscriber – Customer – Brand Advocate.

It can take several touch points before a customer recognizes your name and is aware of what your business can do for them. A marketing funnel is the pathway by which someone goes from Stranger to Brand Advocate. And email marketing is a crucial component that helps you move your readers from one stage to the next in your funnel—from having no awareness to knowing who you are, recognizing what you do, and knowing how your business can help them.

While email should be an integral aspect of your marketing strategy, the premise of this book isn't about growing a big fat email list.

Email marketing is NOT list building alone.

There are several other critical aspects of email marketing. List building is a small portion of this entire book because the quality of subscribers is more important than the quantity. If your email list doesn't drive sales, or if less than 1% of your subscribers are even your ideal customers or have any potential of doing business with you, then it doesn't matter whether you have one thousand or ten thousand subscribers.

I've seen teeny tiny lists earning $4,000 a month and five-figure lists of sixteen thousand subscribers earning the same amount of money. So more does not = better. It's about the relationship you have with your list.

THE 5-STEP ACTIVATION PROCESS

The tips, advice, and strategies presented in this book are not random or ad hoc.

They follow the 5-Step Activation Process below. This process helps you visualize your email marketing as a whole rather than as a bunch of random parts.

It gives you what you need to attract your ideal customers and take them from not knowing who you are to wanting to buy everything you put out for sale.

1. It starts with traffic you send to your website or any page with an incentive or lead magnet (a free resource that you offer in exchange for an email address).

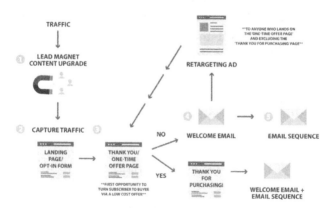

2. You then capture this traffic via a lead capture system such as an opt-in form or landing page.

3. You can then present your new subscriber with a one-time offer or tripwire. This is your first attempt at converting a subscriber into a buyer.

4. Your new subscriber receives your welcome email.

5. Depending on the end goal and pathway you've set out for that subscriber, you will send a dedicated series of emails or follow-up email sequence that primes and nudges that subscriber toward that end goal.

You can have different traffic sources, different entry points for your subscribers (people subscribing via your messenger bot, Facebook page, or Instagram), or different offers you're trying to sell via your email sequence, but the basic flow stays the same.

Steps 1–5 are all you need to get started. You don't necessarily need a bot or to even do ads for that matter. It's these five steps alone that took my business full time and to six figures.

WHAT'S A FUNNEL THEN?

A funnel is nothing but the journey a subscriber takes toward the end goal you've set. It's a strategic, well-thought-out plan that inches the subscriber toward the products and services you offer. You can have an automated webinar funnel that pitches your course. You can also have an evergreen funnel that pitches your e-book or a five-part video series funnel that pitches your membership site.

For all of these you need

1. An entry point (a way for people to enter your funnel) via a lead magnet or any kind of opt-in incentive

2. A way to capture that subscriber via a landing page or opt-in form

3. A dedicated series of emails that prime and nudge that subscriber

Think about it. Isn't this the same as the 5-Step Activation Process above?

IT IS!

Your video series or webinar are extra touch points that you add into your marketing mix.

A funnel (or lack thereof) has become this magic bullet for everything that's likely wrong with a business. So if you've been saying "I need to build more funnels" or "I need a funnel strategist or funnel mentor," I'd like to urge you to stop and think about what exactly it is that you need.

Dig deeper.

Could one of these sentences be more aligned with what's actually going on with your business?

I have thirty thousand page views a month but get only forty-two subscribers for an ENTIRE month. What am I doing wrong? (See section 3 for the answer.)

My email sequence gets a lot of engagement and opens. Everyone says they love my stuff, but I still get no sales for my e-book. Why? (See section 5 for the answer.)

I have a sequence of emails set up in my evergreen funnel, but I'm not getting any sales. Is my product terrible? Should I just scrap it altogether? (See section 7 for the answer.)

These statements allow you to break down and analyze what's wrong rather than throw the burden on the lack of a funnel.

A funnel isn't a physical, tangible thing. It's nothing more than a pathway or journey and one that *you* shape and define. It depends on where *you* want to lead your subscribers.

If you think email marketing is complicated and something you can't do, my goal with this book is to change that opinion.

If you're struggling with any particular aspect of email marketing, this book will give you a fresh perspective on how you can tackle it too.

If this is your first time being introduced to these email marketing terms, it may take some time for all of this to sink in. But I will walk you through each of these five steps in greater detail in the book.

I've deliberately broken down this book into tips and FAQs so that it's an easy read.

FAQs will be interspersed right through the chapters, just like this:

FAQ 1: I have a very tiny email list. Why does email marketing matter to me?

Firstly, a tiny email list is an opportunity. We all start from zero. There are plenty of case studies of people who have had successful launches with a small email list. The most popular being John Meese who generated $10,000 in only 7 days with just 250 subscribers.[6]

Secondly, do the people on your email list know that they are part of a small list? They signed up because they came across something that interested them. Subscribers are the most engaged with your brand in the first forty-eight hours of subscribing.[7] If you follow through when their excitement is most heightened, think about the relationship you'll be building? If you treat your subscribers well, they'll become your first 100 true fans or brand advocates. They'll spread the word about your business and share your content.

FAQ 2: When should I start my email list?

If you haven't launched your business and are working on your site, you should prepare to start your list from the day your site goes live. If you've already launched your business and site, start an email list immediately. If you're ambitious, you don't even have to wait to launch your site. You could create a lead magnet and a landing page and start promoting it.

Again, if you're not familiar with these terms, hang in there because I'll tell you exactly what they mean in just a bit.

Whichever topic you struggle with the most, jump ahead to that section if you must. I don't cover the tech aspect of email marketing in this book, but you do need the following:

1. Email service provider

Your email service provider is an integral aspect of your email and business strategy, so do some shopping around to ensure you pick the right one for your business. Free isn't always the best. I use ConvertKit for my business and wrote a blog post on why I picked ConvertKit vs. Mailchimp[8] when I started, even though I was making $0. Ultimately, it's essential to pick a provider that's not only within your budget but one that's able to grow with your business and that has features and tools to deliver on what you have in mind for your business plans.

2. Lead capture systems

You need a landing page tool as well as a tool that helps you create opt-in forms on your site. I use Thrive Landing Pages and Thrive Leads because these are inexpensive tools with a one-time fee that provide me with hundreds of click and tweak templates. Several email service providers come with these tools built-in as well. I have a tools list within the Email Jumpstart Pack that you can download here >>> https://meera.email/300.

As I say in my emails to my subscribers, I've got your back and you're all set to slay email!

Let's go!

TIPS TO BRAND YOUR EMAIL LIST

What does branding have to do with your email list?

EVERYTHING!

So what is a brand?

It's a set of thoughts, ideas, and emotions that people have about your business. If you're strategic, you can have a heavy hand in shaping the way people think and feel about your brand.

To do that, you need to define what reaction you want your emails to evoke in your subscribers. Curiosity, humor, inspiration, light bulb or "aha" moments, encouragement... What do you want them to get out of your emails? And how does that contribute to your overall brand?

Unlike what most people believe, 64% of subscribers say they are likely to read an email because of *who* it's from. Only 47% attribute it to the subject line. So your name matters more than you think.[9]

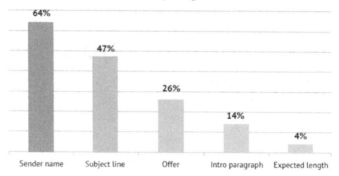

Reasons for opening an email

Image source[9]

This isn't a simple technique or strategy that you can put in place within a day. It takes time to build trust and get subscribers to connect your name with an emotion. There are no shortcuts here.

If you were your own ideal reader, would you want to be on your list? Why or why not?

Here are the questions that you want to answer:

- How do you stand out?

- How are your emails different from others in your niche? What's your unique selling proposition or USP?

- What are 3–5 things you can do or implement to create email content that stands out from the rest?

Your answers should not include tactics such as

I will be consistent…I will send one email a week…I will have a welcome email series…

Your answers should dig deeper into the context and content of your emails.

"70% of my writing goes directly to my list. You're bound to get light bulb and "aha" moments."

That's the USP of my email list. You don't have to state this on your website like I do but knowing exactly how you stand out will help you as you create email content. Your USP is almost like an invisible thread that binds subscribers to your email list.

Think about whose emails you open and why. How are their emails distinct from the others in your inbox?

If you're thinking they provide tons of value…

Sure, they do.

But, don't fall into the value trap.

EVERY EMAIL LIST SHOULD _____

The answer I always get when I ask the above question?

Provide Value.

You're *supposed* to provide value. That's the baseline expectation.

But an email list that stands out isn't necessarily one that's always spoon-feeding subscribers with free tips and resources. I used to think that value was providing free content, free downloads, more free tips and how-tos.

But that couldn't be further from the truth.

The value that makes a difference is being the voice of wisdom for your subscribers...Pointing out their limiting beliefs, mistakes, and myths...Convincing them of your worldview and getting them to buy into it...Turning their assumptions and fears into strength and positivity.

This is what I call value.

Is this more difficult than sending an email with ten must-must-have tips to do something? You bet it is!

These emails can be inspiring, funny, or thought-provoking, and they gel with the brand of the entrepreneur. Not all branded email lists have a similar style. So there isn't one particular way that's best. But reframe what you think value is supposed to mean.

YOU WILL ATTRACT AND REPEL SUBSCRIBERS

Your email list can't be for everyone. People will always unsubscribe no matter how good your emails are. It's not personal.

What you can do:

- **Start by being consistent with your emails**

  That said, don't send an email just for the sake of sending it. Don't compromise on quality just because you *have* to send something out. You can skip a week or two if your emails don't have a strong call to action, or if you have no compelling reason to email your list. While not every email will be your best, make each email count.

- **Be bold and repel (on purpose) if you must**

  Maybe your emails will inspire thought and change. Or challenge existing beliefs and myths. Your content may also raise more questions than it offers answers to. Not everyone jives with that type of content or style.

  But the bolder you are, the more you will attract your ideal reader and repel the rest.

What wouldn't your ideal reader do? What wouldn't they relate to? Identify these characteristics and be as specific as you can; e.g., They are unlikely to read blogs such as…They are unlikely to identify with the term freelancer…They are unlikely to prefer quick tips over long-form content.

Once you have identified these characteristics, keep them in mind as you're working on your email content. Don't water down your message to fit your average reader.

DETERMINE THE ACCESSIBILITY OF YOUR BRAND

Will you encourage subscribers to respond to your emails?

Will you phrase your emails in a way that shows that you value a two-way conversation with your subscribers?

When you do so, you gain tons of insight about what your subscribers are struggling with and what they need you to create for them.

But to do this, you need to be open to responding to your subscribers—either personally or via a team. You can't expect input when you're not willing to participate in the discussion.

As things get more automated, the brands that stand out the most will be those that take a genuine interest in their subscribers. This very much depends on how heavily involved and accessible you want to be. Being very accessible is not part of everyone's brand strategy and that's perfectly ok.

You don't have to be chained to your desk answering emails for hours for this to work. But you need to let people know that there is someone on the other side of your emails.

Here are some steps you can take:

- Have a detailed FAQ page that subscribers can access, with common questions that you always get asked.

- If you don't have a policy of responding to emails personally, or if someone on your team will be responding, or if you only attend to purchase-related emails, make this known clearly on your welcome email. You can also set expectations on your contact form and have an automated email reply.

DETERMINE THE SCOPE OF YOUR EMAILS

By now, you should have a vague idea of what you want your emails to do for your subscribers. This is where you figure out the specifics and determine when and what type of emails you will deliver.

How often should you email your list?

If you have a compelling reason to email your list, go ahead and send an email. Not a straight forward answer, I know. Receiving too many emails is the number one reason why people choose to unsubscribe from an email list.[10] But it's all about being relevant. I've had weeks where I've sent out two or more emails and people didn't leave my list in droves. So it depends on the type of relationship you've built up with your subscribers. Once a week is good for a start. I'll also say this again: if you don't have a good reason to send an email, don't.

What type of emails should you send?

Most people think of an email newsletter.

An email newsletter is an email containing a curation of resources and links to your own posts or external material you think your subscribers will be interested in. If you send one on a weekly basis, your newsletter could be an update for the week. You could also answer questions your readers have in your email. There are several different ways to structure your newsletter.

But an email newsletter is just one type of email. You don't have to send newsletters if you don't want to.

You could send emails focused on a single goal—to get your subscribers to read a blog post, download a lesson, watch a video, or just think about what you shared or reply to it. There are no right or wrong answers to these questions, just what's best for your business and marketing goals as well as your audience.

Here are a few different types of emails you can send:

Common FAQs – An email that answers repeat questions you get from readers and subscribers

Affiliate case study – An email that details the results from taking a course or using a tool that you're an affiliate for

Teaser to an existing post – An email that links to pillar or cornerstone pieces on your blog

Tools and resources – An email that shares your favorite tool collection

The Start Here – An email that links to your most important resources

Break the myths – An email that lays out myths that your subscribers may think are true

Behind the scenes – An email that gives an insiders' peek into what's going on with your business

Personal story – An email that gives an insiders' peek into your struggles or backstory

One-click survey – An email that asks a simple question to segment subscribers or allows them to choose their own email journey

Survey or How can I help you? – An email asking for responses or providing an offer to help

Postpurchase welcome email – An email sent immediately after purchase to buyers of your offer

Unexpected incentive email – A simple cheat sheet, guide, or PDF that subscribers were not expecting

Favorite thing – A collection of your favorite books/blogs/stock photo sites, etc.

I have used every one of these emails in my email marketing mix. Doing so breaks up the monotony of sending the same style of email each week, and each of these emails feeds your marketing goals differently as well.

FAQ 3: How do I pick the right email template?

A template is where your emails come designed with borders, backgrounds, or images. Plain text emails, on the other hand, are what they say they are—just plain text with maybe an occasional image or GIF.

Contrary to what you may believe, you don't need a template. Here's why:

1. Plain text emails have a higher open rate than emails with images.[11] Surprised? While we think visual elements will encourage opens and click-throughs, research across thousands of emails proves otherwise.

2. Plain text emails have a better chance of rendering the way you want them to across different devices. According to a 2017 Litmus Email Client Market Share report,[12] the below image highlights the top email clients based on a study of worldwide email opens. You don't know which platform or device your subscribers will use to check their emails, so you can't guarantee that image-based template emails will display correctly.

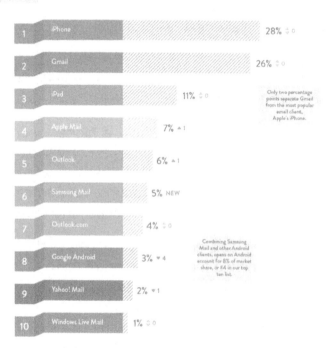

Top Email Clients

The top 10 most popular email clients as of December 2017

iPhone, Gmail, and iPad remained the top 3 email clients in 2017.

Ranking compared to December 2016

1	iPhone	28%
2	Gmail	26%
3	iPad	11%
4	Apple Mail	7%
5	Outlook	6%
6	Samsung Mail	5% NEW
7	Outlook.com	4%
8	Google Android	3%
9	Yahoo! Mail	2%
10	Windows Live Mail	1%

Only two percentage points separate Gmail from the most popular email client, Apple's iPhone.

Combining Samsung Mail and other Android clients, opens on Android account for 8% of market share, or #4 in our top ten list.

Image source[12]

3. An image-dense email also trips up the spam and promotion filters.[13]

Plain text emails aren't suitable for all businesses though, especially e-commerce sites. I absolutely get that. If plain text emails aren't suitable for

24

your brand, make sure that you get your emails professionally coded and formatted. Always run a seed test on a subset of your subscribers to make sure that your emails are landing in the inboxes of your subscribers before you send out your email to your entire list. There are several tools on the market that help with this such as GlockApps and Mailgun but have a chat with your email service provider to see what they recommend and how they can help.

FAQ 4: When should I send my first email?

There's so much pressure on this first email.

If you set up a system even before you get subscribers on to your list, you won't have the first email jitters. There are two emails that you need to have even before you start promoting your lead magnet.

- An email that is sent out immediately after they sign up to deliver your lead magnet

- A welcome email (one at the very least, but if you want to roll out the red carpet for subscribers, I would suggest doing a welcome email series—otherwise known as a nurture sequence—via an autoresponder)

Once you have these set up, you'll have emails going out to your subscribers on auto.

More on how to set up your lead magnet, welcome email, and series in the following sections.

ACTION

What unique benefits do you offer your subscribers by being on your list?

What types of emails will you send?

When will you send your emails? (Frequency + Day/Time)

You can use the worksheets in the Email Jumpstart Pack to help you answer these questions >>> https://meera.email/300.

TIPS TO CREATE A COMPELLING LEAD MAGNET

Opt-in incentive…Opt-in freebie…

Lead magnets go by many names.

A lead magnet is essentially a piece of content that you give a reader for free in exchange for their email address.

BUILDING A LIST OF BUYERS VERSUS FREEBIE HOARDERS

A lead magnet is extremely important in prequalifying your subscriber. The right lead magnet determines whether you get subscribers on your email list who can even be primed to buy your products and services in the first place. It also extensively cuts down the time required to prime them.

Let me explain…

If you're selling an e-book on curriculum and lesson-planning tips specifically for homeschooling, which lead magnet do you think is better?

Lead Magnet A on essential oils or Lead Magnet B on homeschooling teaching plan cheat sheets?

Lead Magnet B prequalifies your audience. The people subscribing to this lead magnet are indicating their interest in this topic. It's much easier to prime an audience who is actively looking for information on this topic than struggle to create an interest link between essential oils and homeschooling.

What if some of those people who subscribed to the lead magnet on essential oils are interested in homeschooling as well?

And can't you get people onto your list and then nurture them?

Sure, both scenarios are possible. But you can't deny that it's harder to establish an interest link.

But why would someone offer a lead magnet on essential oils when they are selling something that's completely different? Is this an exaggerated example?

Well, it happens more often than you think.

Mostly because people don't see the link. They don't see how the different types of lead magnets and content upgrades they have on their site affect the types of subscribers they get and in turn their overall sales.

This is why your lead magnet has to tie in with your business strategy and offers. This makes the difference between building an email list of freebie hoarders or buyers.

GOOD ADVICE: OFFER A LEAD MAGNET THAT ADDRESSES A PAIN POINT

BETTER ADVICE: OFFER A LEAD MAGNET THAT HITS *THESE* 2 POINTS ↓

There are two main things that need to come together to help you decide what lead magnet to create.

1. Alignment with your business and offers

A lead magnet sits at the top of your sales funnel and guides your subscribers to your paid offers. It should not be a disjunct item but rather gel with your offers and content. Alignment is key here and will result in more sales.

I like to reverse engineer the process. Rather than think about pain points immediately, I consider the place of that lead magnet within my business.

What's the purpose of that lead magnet?

Who do you want to attract with that lead magnet and where are you planning on leading them to?

Are you prequalifying subscribers who may potentially be interested in a digital product or service that you're pitching?

If a reader opts in to a lead magnet on writing tips, they are raising their hand and indicating that this is something they are interested in. They probably identify with the need for them to improve in that area. If you nurture them, build trust, and then go on to try to sell them an e-book on essential writing tips, they are more likely to buy your product as opposed to if you pitch them an e-book on productivity tips.

If you have a lead magnet that doesn't lead a subscriber anywhere, is not aligned with your existing offers or future offers, nor does it help position you as an expert or authority on a topic that you want to be known for, then that's a lead magnet that you should potentially consider getting rid of.

2. Place of that lead magnet in your niche

Is your lead magnet unique? Are there similar ones that exist?

While similar lead magnets in your niche are a sign that there's a demand for that lead magnet, you also need to know if that lead magnet is in oversupply. Is your niche tired of seeing that lead magnet? Bloggers and influencers who have a much bigger audience could possibly get away with having something like that, but most of us would do better with a lead magnet that addresses a specific issue or topic.

7 ELEMENTS OF A HIGH CONVERTING LEAD MAGNET THAT GROWS YOUR BUSINESS

1. IT'S EASILY CONSUMABLE

Lead magnets that are simple but pack a punch do a lot better than e-book type freebies that are long and take time to consume. Your readers are already suffocating with information. They don't want a long thirty-page e-book. Your lead magnet should be something they can consume quickly.

2. IT PROVIDES A QUICK WIN

It should be something that gives a quick win or that they can implement quickly. Think instant gratification for your subscriber.

3. IT'S HIGHLY SPECIFIC

Your lead magnet should be highly specific to your target audience and what it helps them achieve.

A strategic lead magnet attracts the right people. Your lead magnet should not be for everybody.

4. IT LEADS YOUR AUDIENCE THROUGH A CHANGE

Every piece of content on your website should bring your audience from A (their current state) to B (their desired state). Likewise, your lead magnet should provide a transformation, no matter how tiny.

5. IT TALKS ABOUT ONE IDEA

Your lead magnet should have one idea or goal as opposed to several ideas.

6. IT ADDRESSES A PROBLEM THEY ARE AL-READY AWARE OF

You can't convince a prospective subscriber of a problem they don't know exists. A lead magnet is one of the first touch points with your brand. Your prospective subscriber needs to know that the problem your lead magnet solves is something they need help with at first glance.

7. IT LEADS TO AN EXISTING/FUTURE PROD-UCT OR SERVICE

You need to have a distinct lead magnet for each product or service (any offer or group of offers) you have on your site.

FAQ 5: If a lead magnet is attracting subscribers but isn't aligned with your business, should you keep it?

Are those subscribers your ideal customers?

Are they likely to do business with you?

Can they be primed to buy your products and services?

These are crucial questions that many fail to consider.

A bigger list isn't necessarily a better one especially if it doesn't justify the cost of maintaining it. Remember the stat I mentioned at the start of the book? For every $1 spent on email marketing, the average return is $44.25. Consider your own return on investment from email. If you're not meeting these numbers, you need to weigh the benefits of attracting subscribers versus the cost of maintaining your email list.

FAQ 6: What's the difference between a content upgrade and a lead magnet?

They are both incentives offered in exchange for an email address. But content upgrades supplement existing pieces of content. For instance, if you have a blog post where you're discussing a specific process to do meal planning, your content upgrade could be a printable of the meal planning schedule or the tools that will help you with meal planning.

ACTION

Consider the lead magnet you have right now and run it against the seven elements above. Does it need a change? You can use the checklist given in the Email Jumpstart Pack >>> https://meera. email/300.

TIPS TO CAPTURE & CONVERT TRAFFIC TO SUBSCRIBERS

Here's a common question I get asked:

Shouldn't I focus on traffic first?

Because if I don't get traffic, I can forget about getting subscribers, right?

Yes and no.

What's not found can't be subscribed to. So if your website leaks traffic and is unable to capture it, no amount of traffic will help you grow your email list.

From conducting webinars to doing live streams, there are several strategies you can employ to grow your email list. I could write an entire book on list-building strategies.

But none of these list-building strategies will make a difference if the lead magnet you have on hand just doesn't work. Or if your opt-in forms and landing pages don't "sell" your lead magnet. Set a solid foundation with your lead magnet, landing page, and website before trying out any list-building or traffic strategy.

As I mentioned at the start, the focus of this book is not list building.

The tips below will focus on bite-sized hacks you can deploy on your website and social media so that both of those channels are optimized to capture traffic. The idea is to make small actions that cumulate to give your list a much-needed boost and set a solid list-building foundation.

WEBSITE

Before you launch a lead magnet, you want to optimize your site as much as possible. Don't be defeated by opt-in blindness. People are "blind" to opt-in forms because they see them in all the usual places. You have to work harder at getting their attention. You can have an attractive lead magnet and still not be able to convert traffic to subscribers because you have a leaky website.

Here are places on your site that you can add an opt-in form to boost your sign-up rate:

- Top bar
- Footer

- Top and bottom of a post

- Exit intent pop-up

- Scroll box

- Below the header or within the header area

- "About me" or "Start here" page (this is one of the most visited pages on your site)

- Resources page

There are plenty of ways to get opt-in forms on your site. Some email service providers provide opt-in forms, but you could also use separate plug-ins like Thrive Leads, Bloom, or PopupAlly.

Use Landing Pages

While opt-in forms are good at capturing readers, they don't have the converting power of landing pages. An opt-in form is usually embedded within a blog post or on a website. Have a look at the diagram below. Think for a second about all the distractions—images, links, sidebar posts, footer, and logos.

A landing page, however, has no navigation bar or external links. Have a look at the diagram below. The focus of a landing page is to get someone to opt in to your lead magnet. This is why my landing pages convert at 30–80% compared to my opt-in forms, which convert between 5–20%. So you definitely want to use landing pages to promote your lead magnets.

Note: The conversion rate is the number of people who sign up for an opt-in incentive divided by the total number of people who visit the opt-in form/landing page, as a percentage.

To craft your landing page effortlessly and not have to stare at a blank template for long, you need the following elements:

- The title of your lead magnet

- The main benefit or main promise of your lead magnet

- What your lead magnet teaches or what your subscribers will learn from it?

  - What will they achieve or overcome by consuming your lead magnet?

- What pain points or problems does your lead magnet solve?

- What desires or motivations does your lead magnet fulfill?

- What mini transformation does it give?

- Testimonials for social proof

- A screenshot, mock-up, or visual of your lead magnet

Note: You want to convert these benefits into 3–7 bullet points. These bullet points should begin with an action verb, with "how to" or "why," or with a number. They should also include specific details such as page numbers or time stamps in videos where key information is found. For example,

- How a 20-minute video recording turned into my first digital product that brought in $36,429.56 in the first month

- 13 limiting beliefs that keep 99% of people from ever launching their ecommerce store—and how to beat them (Hint: You're probably suffering from at least 5 of these) – *pg. 3*

- The ONLY two blogging rules ever (seriously, if you ignore these it will take you YEARS

> to launch your blog and business!) – *1min 37sec*

Your landing page should be a reflection of the words and sentences your target audience uses to describe their pain points. When it does, your target audience recognizes and identifies with the problem. Your lead magnet also becomes immediately more attractive.

Once you have these elements, it's easier to create your landing page.

Add Opt-In Forms or Content Upgrades to Your Top 5–10 Most Trafficked Posts

You can find out what these are by going to Google Analytics > Behavior > Site Content > All Pages.

This gives you a chance to capture the bulk of the traffic that comes to your site even if you don't have the time to add content upgrades to each and every one of your posts. Your opt-in forms should have a mock-up of your content upgrade or lead magnet as well as mention the benefits in attractive bullet points. Here are two examples of opt-in forms on my site.

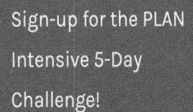

Sign-up for the PLAN Intensive 5-Day Challenge!

- Create 6 Months of content ideas (even more if you're ambitious) in your editorial calendar so you never scramble to publish your content
- Nail down your tasks and goals in detail but making sure they are aligned with your focus for the year
- How to create a **marketing and income plan** for your business with real numbers you can track
- And more!

Email

SIGN ME UP FOR THE CHALLENGE!

NEED HELP CREATING YOUR FIRST (OR NEXT) DIGITAL PRODUCT?

In this guide, you will discover

• When you should NOT create a course and WHAT you should create instead

• 2 criteria that determine how much you can charge for your product

• The No. 1 thing that people pay for and why this is the biggest validation you can do for your product

• The single most important factor in a launch

First Name

Email Address

SEND ME THE GUIDE!

I hate spam as much as you do! Your email's safe here!

Powered by ConvertKit

Add a Link to Your Main Lead Magnets in Your Navigation Bar

Your navigation bar is immediately visible to your site visitors. By adding a heading such as "FREE COURSES" or "FREE REPORT" on your navigation bar, it prompts more people to click through to them.

Create a Subscribe Page

This is a page dedicated to promoting your email list. A subscribe page should have

- A strong headline that states the benefits of your email list.

- An indication of what they can expect to receive in return for their email address. If it's a digital report or guide, a mock-up or image of it should also appear.

- A sample or two of the emails that you actually send out. (Optional)

Here's a link to my subscribe page: http://www. meerakothand.com/blogging-strategy/.

Use Your 404 Page to Build Your Email List

Broken links can scare potential readers away from your website. Get a plug-in like 404page—a smart custom 404 error page that allows you to change a WordPress page into a custom 404 page. Then add an opt-in form on the page.

MAKE SHARING YOUR POSTS RIDICULOUSLY EASY

The more you get your posts in front of people, the easier it will be for new readers to subscribe.

Add Click to Tweets within Your Blog Posts

Click to tweets are quotes or punchy sentences within each post. If you use the Social Warfare plug-in, you can easily create click to tweet boxes within your posts like I've done here. You can also do so by downloading the free Click to Tweet plug-in.

Add Share Links to Emails, Thank-You Pages, and within Lead Magnets

Here's how you add share links:

Facebook – http://www.facebook.com/sharer/sharer.php?u=INSERT YOUR LINK

It's as simple as that. You can hyperlink that link to a word, Facebook icon, or image. Whenever someone clicks on it, the Facebook window will open up with your image and link.

Twitter – Head to Bit.ly and shorten the URL of your landing page. Then head to Click to Tweet and type in a custom tweet.

See how I've done it on this thank-you page.

KEEP PEOPLE ON YOUR SITE LONGER BY ADDING RELATED POSTS

The longer your readers are on your site, the higher the chances of them signing up for a content upgrade or a lead magnet.

Add UpPrev

This is a free plug-in that recommends a post to your readers at the bottom of the page. This is how it looked on my old site.

Add Related Posts

I use Related Posts by Zemanta, which adds images of related posts right at the end of the post. See the image below. Another similar plug-in you can use is Contextual Related Posts.

KEEP READING...

ARE YOU NEW & UNKNOWN? HERE ARE 15 HACKS THAT GIVE YOU INSTANT EXPERT STATUS	HOW THIS BLOGGER GREW HER NEW BLOG TO OVER 20K PAGE VIEWS IN JUST 3 MONTHS	NO TIME TO WRITE? THIS TEMPLATE & PROCESS CUT MY WRITING TIME BY 50%

Make Use of White Space by Adding a Sticky Sidebar Widget

How do you make use of the white space in a sidebar after a reader scrolls down a certain portion of the page? You can do this by adding a sticky widget such as the Q2W3 Fixed Widget. After activating the plug-in, go to Appearance » Widgets and click on the widget that you want to make sticky. This will give you a sticky, floating widget that follows along the length of the page with the reader.

Remove Categories from Your Sidebar for New Blogs

If your blog is new and you don't have a lot of posts, don't add categories to your sidebar. When a user clicks through, it doesn't reflect well when there are only one or two posts in each category. Don't clutter your sidebar with several opt-ins, banners, or affiliate products. When you give readers too many options, they take none.

Remove Unnecessary Widgets

Avoid adding unnecessary widgets like Facebook or Pinterest widgets that make the reader click away from your site.

Share Landing Pages in PR Activities

If you're doing a guest post or are featured on a podcast, share a landing page in your author bio rather than your home page link so that you convert more new readers to subscribers.

SOCIAL MEDIA

Add Your Landing Page Links to Your Social Media Profiles and Pages

Rather than send people to your home page, leave a link to your landing page or subscribe page in your social media profiles.

Share Your Lead Magnet on Social Media

Don't just share your articles and posts on social media. Make separate images for your lead magnets and share those as well. Create a description of your lead magnet and share it within Facebook group promotion or share threads. The link you want to send people to is your landing page link.

FACEBOOK

Add a Sign-Up Form to Your Facebook Business Page

You've probably noticed the call to action button appearing under your cover photo.

This button can be customized to show a variety of calls to action such as "Send Message," "Contact Us," "Sign Up," and more. Simply hover over the button, select "Edit Button," then click "Sign Up." You'll now be asked to provide a link to your landing page, and that's it!

Now whenever someone clicks on the "Sign Up" button, they'll be taken directly to your landing page.

Promote Your Lead Magnet on Your Facebook Cover Photo

Your cover photo is one of the most valuable pieces of real estate you have on your Facebook page. I've seen several entrepreneurs promote their lead magnet on this cover page with a captivating image and a short link. This link directs readers away from Facebook and on to your site.

PINTEREST

Share Your Lead Magnet on Pinterest

The pin image that you share does not need to be one that's found on your website. You can create 2–3 separate vertical pins promoting your lead magnet. Write a compelling description with keywords. Head over to your Pinterest profile, find the "plus" sign and upload your image. Link the image to your landing page.

Home Following Meera Kotha...

Here are three examples of pin images that lead to landing pages. These take readers away from Pinterest directly to my landing pages.

TWITTER

Promote Your Lead Magnet on Your Twitter Cover Photo

FAQ 7: I have thirty thousand page views a month but get vonly forty-two subscribers for

an ENTIRE month. What am I doing wrong?

What's important in list building isn't the different tactics you use but your list building foundation. Here's what I mean by foundation:

1. Are potential subscribers familiar with the words you've used on your landing page and opt-in forms? Can your audience see themselves in the problem you're describing?

2. Is this something they want (NOT need)?

   Does your opt-in incentive solve a burning pain point or is it something *you* think they need? Do they immediately recognize that they need this?

3. Do the words used on the call to action button prompt action or does the button say "Subscribe Now"? (I've seen several sites that still use the Subscribe Now button)

4. Is your site optimized?

   Traffic is good. But are you able to convert that traffic into subscribers?

5. Do you have a landing page with an attractive headline and does it clearly spell out the benefits of the lead magnet?

A landing page is distraction-free which means you'll be able to convert more traffic, but you need to have a compelling and attractive headline.

So there are lots of things that could be wrong, and you may need to analyze the issue on a few fronts. Have a look at your opt-in forms and landing pages and run them through these points. What do you need to improve on? Where are you stuck?

ACTION

1. Where are you missing out on opportunities to grow your list? For example, posts with no content upgrade, no opt-in incentive?

2. What methods will you use to capture traffic from your site?

- Footer

- Exit intent pop-up

- Top bar

- Sidebar

- Header

- Below the header

- About page

- Resources/tools page

- Top and bottom of every blog post

- Others

3. What channels will you use to promote your email list? **Note:** If you're starting out, pick one platform first. Once you're getting a steady number of subscribers from that source, move on to work on another platform. Don't spread yourself too thin by working on multiple platforms at the same time.

- Pinterest

- Facebook

- Twitter

- LinkedIn

- Instagram

- Influencer outreach

- Guest posting

- Others

TIPS TO CREATE A BRAND-BOOSTING WELCOME EMAIL

We've covered the first three steps of the 5-Step Activation Process.

You're now equipped to create a lead magnet and optimize your site to capture and convert traffic to subscribers. This is where a new reader becomes a subscriber, and one of the first communications they receive from you is the welcome email.

Welcome emails have the highest open rates among all emails[14] with the average open rate for welcome emails being 50%[15]. But most welcome emails don't do a brand any justice largely because of the following seven reasons.

7 THINGS YOUR WELCOME EMAIL MUST DO (BUT PROBABLY DOESN'T!)

1. Your welcome email sounds completely different from your other content

56

Your brand has a voice. It's the tone you use to communicate with your audience. And that voice is infused into your content and your interaction with your readers.

The words, tone, and style you use in your content say a lot about your brand.

Your subscribers likely read a few of your blog posts or watch a couple of videos before opting in to your email list. And when they do, are they getting the same brand experience? Or do you sound like a completely different person?

Most people clamp up when it comes to writing emails, but an email is just like a blog post.

It's an extension of your brand. So a consistent brand voice is essential.

2. Your welcome email doesn't state why you are the best person to help them

It doesn't matter what niche your business is in. Most of our businesses exist to entertain, educate, or inspire our readers and customers.

Identify the purpose of your business:

- Are you educating a reader about healthy eating?

- Are you inspiring him/her to fix her money mindset?

- Are you educating your reader about how he/she can travel the world on a shoestring budget?

Now that you have identified this, why are you the best person to inspire, educate, or teach your subscriber about this?

This is where lots of people have hesitations about not being an expert. You don't need to be an expert. You don't need to have a certification or be blogging for an insanely long period of time. You don't need to earn six figures or be an author as well.

You just need to be two steps ahead of your reader or ideal customer.

Are there certain things you did that made you clear your college debt within three years? Have you slashed your grocery budget through meal planning? Have you visited more than ten countries on a limited budget?

While these may seem ordinary to you, there are people who would love to do some of what you've done. So share your experiences in your welcome email and give them a glimpse of what they can learn from you and what *change* they can expect by reading your content.

If you've been featured on high profile sites or podcasts, this is also your tiny space to let your new subscriber know about it. They need to know you're a trusted source, so don't hesitate to share your achievements, no matter how small.

3. Your welcome email does not hint at an invitation to converse with you

You may have heard about the importance of asking your subscriber *"What are you struggling with?"*

This phrase was popularized by Derek Halpern of Social Triggers, and you may have seen several of your favorite bloggers asking the same question in their emails.

While that very term *"What are you struggling with?"* is getting pretty clichéd, the principle behind it is to encourage the reader to share their thoughts with you. By opening a conversation loop, you invite feedback and are able to peek directly into what your subscriber needs. This gives you insight into the content and products you possibly can offer.

But what can you ask without sounding like 95% of the online entrepreneurs out there?

If you're a travel blogger, you could ask them what region or country they want to conquer next and what their biggest hurdles are with traveling.

If your business is about organic living, you could ask them what questions they have about shopping for organic food.

Your question has to be simple and specific to your niche. You can do this in the postscript or P.S. of your email.

But be prepared to get replies. And if you want to nurture your audience, respond to as many of those emails as you can. We spoke briefly about brand accessibility in section 1. If you don't intend to be accessible via email, set expectations right from the start.

4. Your welcome email promises you won't send too many emails

I've seen this in several welcome emails I've reviewed. Yes, you're being considerate of your subscribers' time and space. But these new subscribers opted in because they like your content and feel that you can help them. Why would they not want your emails especially if this is something they opted in to?

Your audience will unsubscribe if they're not comfortable with your email frequency. But this shouldn't be a reason to email your list any less especially if you have a good reason to email them.

5. Your welcome email sounds like a goodbye

Will I hear from you again?

Will I only get updates?

Is this goodbye?

Several welcome emails I've reviewed don't give the reader a glimpse of what's coming next?

Will they get more emails? What are you going to be sharing?

A welcome email is a conversation. You want them to think about things and look forward to seeing your name in their inbox. This works best when you have a nurture sequence that follows your welcome email. More on that in the next section.

6. Your welcome email does not tease and intrigue

How do you make your subscriber anticipate your next email? How do you get them to look out for your name in their inbox? How do you keep them on edge thinking about something you raised?

You can do so by adding a dash of tease and intrigue in your welcome email.

Close your email with a question. Here are some examples of how to do this:

Do you know that 90% of what people believe about organic vegetables is wrong? I'll tell you what that myth is tomorrow and how it's going to help you cut your expenditure by up to 50%.

Do you know how long it takes for your body to form a habit? The answer will shock you. Look out for that tomorrow.

When you tease, you also need to ensure that you close the loop in the next email.

7. Your welcome email has too many asks

Help me with a survey

What product should I create?

What blog posts should I write?

While it's not wrong to ask your audience to help you with something, an ask made too soon or an ask that is clearly only beneficial to you is a huge NO.

It can also be downright repulsive.

Likewise, think carefully about the links you place in your welcome email.

Which social platforms are most important to you? Where do you want them to follow you? What do you want them to do?

Choose your links accordingly so that the reader takes the action that you want them to take.

Giving too many choices ends up being counterproductive and it confuses the reader.

ACTION

Have a look at your welcome email now. Have you included the following?

- Explained who you are and what you do

- Explained why you are the best person to learn from

- Described what they can expect from you

- Asked them to follow you on 1–2 social media platforms

- Opened a curiosity loop (in the P.S.) about what your next email will be about

- Asked a specific question and encouraged a reply

TIPS TO NURTURE NEW SUBSCRIBERS ON AUTO WITH A WELCOME EMAIL SERIES/NURTURE SEQUENCE

A welcome email series is nothing but an email sequence that's sent on auto based on a frequency and order that you predetermine.

Email sequences have a multitude of benefits.

Each email in your sequence can build off the previous one to help reinforce your brand and get your subscribers acquainted with your best content, what you have to offer, and why you're the best person to help them. It can help pitch and sell your product on auto. It also allows you to establish a relationship with your subscriber and build trust.

WHAT GOES INTO A WELCOME EMAIL SERIES/ NURTURE SEQUENCE?

There isn't a fixed answer to this, and it depends largely on your end goal.

Do you have an offer you'd like to pitch? Do you want them to get on a discovery call with you? Are you trying to instill a mindset change? Are you inviting them to your free community?

Every single subscriber who enters your list has multiple pathways that they can take. The possibilities and combinations are endless. You decide how to lead them and where you're leading them toward. **The pathway you set, though, should be steered by relevancy**.

Is the sequence relevant to the lead magnet or content upgrade that a subscriber subscribed to? Is the lead magnet that the subscriber subscribed to relevant to the content that they were reading or viewing?

The higher the degree of relevance between every single component, the higher your engagement, sales, and overall subscriber satisfaction. The way you pave these pathways will determine whether (a) your offers (products and services) get maximum eyeballs, (b) the people who enter a sequence or pathway are the most likely to be interested in the offer you're pitching at the end, and (c) the people entering the sequence will even care about your message. This requires careful thought and analysis on your part.

This is where it's useful to map out all the touch points a subscriber potentially has with your brand.

Potential subscribers come in contact with your brand via various channels or touch points like I mention in my book *Your First 100*. Here are just a few possibilities:

- Instagram

- Facebook groups

- Pinterest

- Twitter

- Guest post bio

- Roundup post through another blog

- Live streaming link

- Mention via another blog

- Subscribe page on social media

Knowing the various ways subscribers may subscribe to your list would mean that you have no open loops or holes. Every subscriber is taken care of no matter how they come into your system—whether it's through a different opt-in offer or a different link.

CHOOSING THE PATHWAY

But how do you determine the pathway a subscriber takes?

What makes the most sense to your business model?

If you primarily have digital products, you might find it useful to group content, lead magnets, and sequences according to offers. This means that you may have different sequences for each offer.

If you primarily benefit from sponsored posts or ad revenue, you may find it useful to group lead magnets and sequences according to topics.

When you're starting out, it may be fairly straightforward because you may not have extensive content upgrades or lead magnets.

But having a good foundation in place is important so that you don't accidentally leave out a group of subscribers from receiving your welcome email or welcome email series. Or leave out a group of people who stumble across a post or page that doesn't have an opt-in form.

Here are three likely scenarios:

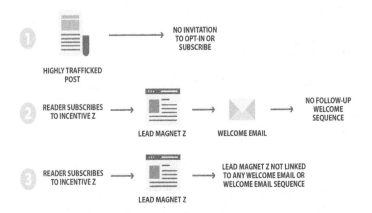

What if you're just getting started?

If you have no offers, you could set up a sequence of emails for each content category like I talk about in my book *One Hour Content Plan*. Then your welcome email series can introduce subscribers to your brand, your best content, and the value you provide. Point them to existing pieces of content that give a glimpse into what you believe in. You can also share your personal story.

By the end of the welcome email series, you will have created a solid foundation and impression of your work and delivered as much value as you possibly can. This is a trial to show them what they can expect by being on your list and how you can help them.

It takes some time to set up these emails, but once you do, your nurture sequence is a tool that's going to help you nurture your list on auto.

Imagine every subscriber going through an onboarding sequence that introduces them to your brand, your best content, and the value you provide. Imagine the impression that would make on your subscribers. Your new subscribers will be taken care of no matter when they opt in to your list. Even if that's during the holiday season or when you're on vacation.

Most of my students and clients (including me!) start by having a general welcome email series. Over time, as your business models and offers become clearer and more refined, your email sequences can become increasingly targeted with clear end goals.

WRITING THOSE SCARY SEQUENCE EMAILS

What you include in your email sequence will very much depend on the goal of your sequence. An email sequence is there to **nudge** subscribers toward this very end goal that you've set.

To nudge subscribers is to

- Make your audience aware that they have a problem that needs to be solved

- Get them to view you as an expert and trust you with the subject

- Get them to understand the solution and benefits of solving the problem

- Remove objections they have about the offer

- Build anticipation for your upcoming offer

When you do all of these and you pitch your offer at the end, you are more likely to bag a sale or get your subscriber taking action on that end goal that you've set than someone who doesn't think through their email sequence strategically.

In the *One Hour Content Plan* as well as *Your First 100,* I mention the customer journey. You'll get readers who are at different ends of the spectrum or different parts of the customer journey. Some may have no clue about the problem your business or offer helps to solve. Some may be actively searching for a solution to it and comparing different products and services on the market. Look at the table below for the five different states of awareness.

A subscriber is likely to be **Problem Unaware** if they haven't yet identified their pain or problem

A subscriber is likely to be **Problem Aware** if they are aware of what they need help with

A subscriber is likely to be **Solution Unaware** when they've felt pain but have not discovered that solutions exist for it (have not started "shopping around")

A subscriber is likely to be **Solution Aware** when they know that a problem exists, and they have discovered that solutions exist for it (they have started "shopping around")

A subscriber is likely to be **Most Aware** when they are aware of a problem that needs to be solved and how your offer helps them solve it

Your email sequence needs to bring attention to the problem, instill desire for the solution, and remove your subscribers' objections. If subscribers are not convinced that they have a problem that needs solving—if they have objections that your offer won't work for them—then they are unlikely to take action.

Sending these subscribers to your sales page is a conversion killer.

Every single email in a sequence is a little milestone marker and has to inch them forward. If you still have problems in this area, think of your emails as a thread. They have to nudge your subscribers along a journey. What do they have to know first? What do they need to know next? Your emails should help connect the dots with what you're trying to help them achieve.

Have you done enough to justify the ask?

FAQ 8: My email sequence gets a lot of engagement and opens. Everyone says they love my stuff, but I still get no sales for my e-book. Why?

There are a few things that could be going on here.

Firstly, when I started my business, someone who was further along in the journey said, "Sell to them soon. If not, when you do, they're going to start unsubscribing in droves."

While I don't completely agree with this statement, the underlying thought is that subscribers need to get used to you asking. We refer to it as a call to action, but I like to see it as a **microcommitment.**

These are tiny steps that a subscriber can take to show that they are still interested in what you have to say—that they aren't just passive readers. Taking a survey, replying to your email, or sharing your work are examples of microcommitments. When they get used to you asking for small commitments, they will get used to you asking for the sale as well. Are you getting your subscribers to make microcommitments?

Secondly, are you priming them for the sale? Is your free content related to the topic of your offer? If your answer is no, you likely have people who aren't interested in the problem your offer solves or who need to move further down the awareness spectrum to be ready to say YES to your offer.

Thirdly, are you providing too much free value? Too much free value can be harmful. It doesn't inspire action or commitment from your audience. Think back to what we discussed about value in section 1.

Lastly, are you selling the benefits or features in your email? Nobody wants the "thing" or offer you're selling. People don't pay for the features of your offer. They pay for what they think will help them achieve and the outcomes. Sell the other side of the river and not the stepping stones. No one wants a website, but they will pay for it if they want the outcomes of a great converting website or to avoid the pain of creating one themselves.

Are your sales emails and calls to action painting a picture of the other side or are they focused on selling the features of your offer? When in doubt, add a "so that" behind your sentences to ensure your features are followed by the benefits your subscribers will enjoy.

FAQ 9: Is seven the magic number of emails you need in an email sequence?

It's a common marketing principle that it takes seven touches before someone is ready to act on your call to action. But this doesn't necessarily mean that it takes seven emails to get a sale. How can seven be a blanket number for every single business model or offer available?

Let's say you have a $3,000 offer and a $100 offer. Would they both take the same number of emails to convince the person to take you up on it?

I'm guessing no.

The more complex your offer, the more objections, false beliefs, and assumptions you need to help your subscriber overcome. That's what an email sequence is for. A sequence is there to nudge your subscriber.

Not an automation tool you need to have because everyone says so...Not a place to have your subscribers bursting out of the seams with value in the form of free downloads or checklists...

(I fell for this one. It actually works in the opposite way. More free stuff doesn't quite = more sales.)

So the magic number isn't seven as much as everyone would like you to believe. The magic is knowing how to work back on your emails to get the sale!

ACTION

1. If you have existing products and services, does each one have a subscriber pathway?

2. Take a look at your email sequence and individual emails. With this content, are subscribers ready to take action on your sequence end goal (the one you determined at the start)?

   • Have you asked for microcommitments from your audience? (Got them to reply to your emails, got them to sign up for something, or got them to raise their hands and say they're interested?)

   • Is your call to action clear at the end of your sequence? Do subscribers know without a doubt what they're supposed to do?

   • Does your email sequence remove objections and false beliefs that subscribers may have?

TIPS TO FILL YOUR EMAIL EDITORIAL CALENDAR

The biggest complaint:

What should I send? I don't have enough original content on top of blog posts.

This is why you need an email editorial calendar. Just as you would have an editorial calendar for your blog content, you should have one for your email marketing content.

Solopreneurs struggle to come up with email ideas because they see email as a separate entity. Email is just another arm of your content marketing efforts. Your blog and email editorial calendar should feed off one another. The sooner you tie your email list into your marketing plan, the easier it is to come up with content ideas.

3 WAYS TO PLAN YOUR EMAIL CONTENT

1. Plan your email content around offers and promotions in your marketing calendar

Rather than show up on the day of your launch and tell your subscribers to buy your offer, you can create a simple nurture and prime campaign leading up to your promotion or cart open date.

If you have an affiliate promotion on August 25 for instance, you need to prime your audience 2–3 weeks ahead so that they have all the information they need to say YES to your offer.

2. Create monthly themes (for beginners who have no offers)

Having a theme makes it so much easier to organize and come up with ideas. This is how most magazines structure their content. They have editorial calendars that are broken up into monthly themes and they organize their content based on that. For instance, August is back to school; January is about New Year's resolutions and goals; February is about relationships. The emails surrounding a theme go on to become an email campaign.

3. Set goals

Is there a topic you're trying to establish expertise in? Do you want to test a product or service idea by sharing content around it with your audience? Plan your email content around your goals. By stacking your email content together with your other content channels (be it a blog post or a podcast or a video), you will achieve that goal faster.

I suggest having an email editorial calendar for three months. If you send one email a week, that works out to only twelve emails that you need to brainstorm ideas for. Block out a time where you write your emails. This ensures you stay consistent.

If you need an editorial calendar that doubles up for email and your blog, check out the CREATE Planner.

YOUR SEQUENCE IS NOT THE ONLY TYPE OF EMAIL YOU SEND

There are two main email types or vehicles—sequences and broadcasts. The type of content in both is inherently different.

Broadcasts are used for

- Time-sensitive content

- Live launches or promotional emails

Sequences are used for

- Evergreen launches or funnels

- Onboarding

- Nurture emails after sign-up to email list

Both have a place in your marketing system.

You concurrently can have new subscribers going through your welcome email series (or nurture sequence) and send broadcast emails with time-sensitive promotions to subscribers who have completed your nurture sequence.

BEST PRACTICES

1. Keep new subscribers who are going through your welcome email series or nurture sequence out of your promotional emails. Imagine being just a day old on someone's email list and being bombarded with launch content on an offer you know nothing about. Nothing makes a subscriber hit unsubscribe faster than being in a situation like that.

2. Always have an identification or tagging system to know which subscribers have completed a sequence and which are actively going through a sequence.

3. Ensure that subscribers do not receive the same welcome email and sequence twice. This could happen if they sign up for another free resource on your site that is linked to the same email sequence.

FAQ 10: How do I prevent people from unsubscribing from my emails?

Not all unsubscribes are bad. You should welcome the unsubscribe if you know you've been consistently providing value to your list. An engaged list of buyers or potential buyers is what you need, not a bigger one.

Here are a couple of reasons why people unsubscribe:

- **They receive too many emails**

  Not every subscriber will have a similar appetite to email frequency. Like I mentioned earlier on in the book, if you have a reason to send those emails, go ahead and send them without worrying about who will unsubscribe. But here's something you need to note. Are you sending emails on vastly different topics? If so, can you segment your list or get subscribers to specify their preferences?

- **Their direction or focus has changed, and your emails are not relevant to them anymore**

  It's best to let these subscribers go. You'd rather have them unsubscribe than mark you as spam or stay dormant on your list.

- **They are at a different experience level than your target audience**

  Do you see yourself creating targeted content for this group of subscribers? If you don't intend to serve this group of subscribers because it doesn't make sense for your business, that's perfectly fine. Embrace the unsubscribe.

- **They can't remember how they got on your list in the first place**

  You need to ensure that you're top of mind so that subscribers can recognize your name and brand. But you shouldn't have this issue if you have a welcome email and nurture sequence set up from the start.

FAQ 11: How do I make sure I don't land in the junk folder?

Every email sender has a sender reputation given by the mailbox providers. The more engaged your list is and the higher your opens are, the better your chances of landing in your subscribers' primary email tabs and not in the junk or promotions folders. The more unsubscribes, unopens, and email bounces you get from your recipients, the lower your score will be. This is why it's so important to clean your email list. I tell you exactly how to clean your list in Section 8.

FAQ 12: Should I send blog post notifications?

If there's nothing else you're sending your list, then sending blog post notifications is better than sending nothing at all. At least, you're showing up in your subscribers' inboxes and continuing to be top of mind. But if a blog post notification is the only thing your subscribers see that you're sending, they're going to start tuning you out in due time. Your emails become predictable but for the wrong reason. Your emails will not evoke any particular emotion with your subscribers like we discussed in section 1.

FAQ 13: It's been three months since I sent an email to my list. What should I do and what should I send them?

You need to be prepared for what will definitely happen—the unsubscribes. The extent of your unsubscribes will depend on the goodwill and relationship you had with your list prior to when you went missing.

If your content has made an impact on them...

If you were relatively consistent before...

If you also have a welcome email series that has been nurturing subscribers on auto even throughout your hiatus, then you don't have to worry much.

But if you have no relationship with your list, then brace yourself for the unsubscribes. I've given you an email template below that you can send out to your email list. I also suggest including an incentive that you can offer to compensate for going missing. If you have a main opt-in incentive where most of your subscribers have come in from, offer an incentive that's related to that. This way, the incentive you offer will *speak* to your subscribers.

These are people who've raised their hands and told you they are interested in this topic by signing up for it. So give them more of what they asked for. This could be an exclusive guide, report, cheat sheet, or checklist.

It's also a way of communicating the value you provide. You're reminding them of what they signed up for in the first place.

Another incentive you can offer is a free call or service offer. I'd suggest offering this as a complement to your guide or report because there are limits to the number of free calls you can possibly do. And you want each and every one of your subscribers to feel like they got value out of what you sent—you want them to have a piece of what you're giving. That works best with a download of some kind.

TEMPLATE

SUBJECT LINE: I messed up/Sorry! Let's be friends?/Can I help you?/Free call/

Hey, [FIRST NAME GOES HERE]!

It's been [X] months since I last sent you an email. I'll be the first to admit it—that's not right.

I needed some time to [reconsider my business direction/rebrand/move across the country/work on things].

===>> If they may have no clue who you are, put in this paragraph.

If you're scratching your head wondering who I am, I don't blame you. I'm [introduce your business/ brand and who you are]. You most likely signed up for [name of your incentive].

I value your time and I appreciate you for giving me space in your inbox.

To say thank you and to make it up to you, please download this exclusive [guide/report/cheat sheet/ checklist] on [topic]. In this [guide/report/cheat sheet/checklist], you will discover

- Bullet point 1

- Bullet point 2

- Bullet point 3

I'm also giving away five thirty-minute one-on-one [what service do you provide? Pinterest/branding/design/productivity planning?] consultations.

This will be a live Skype call where I answer any questions you have on [X].

If this is something you need right now, hit reply to this email and answer one quick question: What's your biggest struggle with [X] right now?

At the end of the day, I'll go through the responses, pick five, and notify you.

What's the catch?

There isn't one. I'm not going to waste thirty minutes of your time and then pitch you on a paid session or product of some type.

You can be assured I'm not going to pitch you anything.

Thank you so much. I'm really looking forward to reading your responses.

ACTION

Which dates are important for your business? Do you have an email strategy around your key business dates?

TIPS TO MONETIZE YOUR EMAIL LIST

The simplest way to monetize your email list immediately is to employ a tripwire strategy.

A tripwire is a low-ticket product usually offered as soon as someone signs up to your email list. Tripwires are usually e-books, mini-guides, videos, audio files, templates, cheat sheets, or reports. Your product should preferably be under $50. I've seen tripwires at various price points from $7, $17, $29, and $39.

Though the price is low, the product should be high in value.

Studies say that people are more likely to buy from you a second time if they've done it before. The idea behind a tripwire is to get more people to open their wallets for you. To get more buyers on your list—not just subscribers. It's meant to showcase your expertise.

Creating your product is the most time intensive aspect of the tripwire. I'm not going to cover product creation in this book. But for more information, you can sign up for my free email course Get Product Ready here » meerakothand.com/get-product-ready/.

There are 5 (+1) aspects of a tripwire strategy:

1. A simple product

2. A simple sales page

3. A pathway

4. Urgency—an evergreen timer

5. File delivery + payment processor

6. Retargeting ad *This is an optional step. It helps to maximize your sales but is not a must if you don't have a budget for ads*

You can put a pixel on your sales page and thank-you page after someone purchases your tripwire. You can then run a simple Facebook retargeting ad to everyone who lands on your sales page and exclude people who landed on your thank-you page (because they've already purchased).

This retargeting ad can remind them of the benefits they missed out on by not purchasing the tripwire.

Here's an example of how this looks:

The most critical element of a tripwire strategy is the pathway.

Once you have your product and sales page, you need to think about how you're going to get people to that sales page to view your tripwire offer. There are different ways you can introduce your tripwire to your subscriber.

- You can do it as soon as they opt in.

  Plot out which blog posts are closely related to the tripwire product you created. Once you have this mapped out, create a content upgrade or free resource readers can opt in to on those posts.

Redirect them to a sales page or thank-you page once they opt in to the free resource. This is easy to set up in any email service provider.

Give instructions to your subscriber. Why are they seeing this sales page and where's their download? Have a sentence at the very top of the tripwire sales page to address this. I've given an example of my tripwire page below.

- You can also introduce your tripwire via an email sequence or email course.

Thank you for signing up! Your download/first lesson is hurtling its way to your inbox but...

While You're Here, Want to Grab My Entire Email Marketing Template Pack for just $17?

Includes **word-for-word** scripts, tested and proven email templates & optimized email subject lines to boost **more sales** and engagement **in less time**

$$00 : 14 : 16$$
hours   minutes   seconds

Notice how many course creators say that their sales rolled in at the last hour? That's because the ticking clock pushes people to make a purchasing decision.

Urgency is a good sales tool. Expiring bonuses, price increases, and time-sensitive offers are a few ways to create urgency. For tripwires, because of their low price point, time sensitivity is the easiest way to create urgency. You want to include a countdown timer to inject this urgency. But what is key here is an evergreen countdown timer. An evergreen countdown timer is one that is not tied to a date or time.

This means that two different people can sign up for the same resource in January or July and both of them will still be shown the tripwire sales page. This usually works through cookies or by identifying their IP address.

So even if they access the page via a different browser, the timer doesn't start afresh but redirects to an expired page or to a sales page with the tripwire being offered at the "original" or higher price if the initial timer has lapsed.

Deadline Funnel and Thrive Ultimatum are examples of paid plug-ins that give you the option of having evergreen countdown timers.

SELL EVERGREEN PRODUCTS VIA AN EVERGREEN FUNNEL (A.K.A PATHWAY)

Evergreen products are those that are always available for sale and are not tied to launches or open and close carts. These are usually offered for sale via an evergreen funnel or pathway. Here's an example of how an evergreen funnel could look.

Blog post (with content upgrade) » Thank-you page » Email sequence of ten emails with an offer to buy Product A » Simple retargeting ad

Here are the aspects behind an evergreen funnel strategy:

- An evergreen product
- A sales page
- A pathway
- A sequence of emails
- Urgency—an evergreen timer
- Offer delivery + payment processor
- Retargeting ad *This is an optional step*

You can add evergreen webinars, workshops, and videos into the mix if you'd like, but the basic elements are what you see above.

FAQ 13: I have an evergreen email sequence, but I'm not getting any sales. Is my product terrible? Should I just scrap it altogether?

Before you decide to scrap your product, there are a few things you need to consider:

1. Do you have enough people going through your funnel?

Sales conversion rates can vary from 1–8% with 2–3% being the average. This means that 2% of people who go through that funnel will end up purchasing your product. This number differs for a lot of people and possibly differs between niches. But you need a certain volume of people going through your funnel before you decide that it's not converting for you.

2. Have you done enough to justify the ask?

Have you brought attention to the problem, raised interest, and instilled desire for your product? Your email sequence has to do all of these before your reader is going to even consider saying yes to your ask.

3. Are there sufficient pathways to get eyeballs on your product?

Imagine that there is one single entry point for a subscriber to get onto an email sequence, and that's via a content upgrade on a single blog post. How many people do you think will get their eyeballs on your evergreen product? Not many. Especially if that blog post is not heavily trafficked or optimized to capture subscribers. The more pathway entry points you have, the more opportunities you have for someone to subscribe and the more eyeballs you get on your offer.

4. Are you testing your emails?

From which emails do you have a drop in open and click-through rates? Different audiences respond to different types of email content and subject lines. Does your audience respond better to video? Then host your files on Vimeo, Wistia, or YouTube and have a screenshot of the video in the email that links directly to it. This gives the subscriber a compelling visual to click on. Do you need to shorten your emails? Include a more enticing postscript to keep them glued to your sequence? Being aware of these factors will help you tweak your content or subject lines.

If subscribers are not in your sequence long enough and drop off even before you introduce the offer, then your sales don't stand a chance. Switch things up and make tweaks as you analyze your stats. It will take time though before you hit the sweet spot.

ACTION

Where are you missing out on opportunities to make more sales from your email list?

Section 8

TIPS TO MEASURE YOUR EMAIL PERFORMANCE

The most common email metrics are open and click-through rates.

An open rate is the percentage of people who opened your email from the total that received it. According to a HubSpot study,[16] analyzing more than twenty-five million emails across twenty-eight industries, the average open rate was found to be 32% with Marketing and Advertising companies having the lowest email open rates and Arts & Entertainment, Construction, Human Resources, Legal & Government, and Real Estate having the highest open rates. According to a Mailchimp Email Marketing Benchmarks study of its customers, the average open rate was 20.81%.[17]

If you have a good open rate, it usually means (a) your subject lines resonate with your audience, (b) your audience is familiar with your name and brand, and (c) they associate your brand name with an emotion or value.

Your click-through rate is the percentage of people who clicked on a link in your email from the total number of people who opened it. The click-through rate reveals how people are responding to the content of your email—if they find your content relevant enough to click through for more. The same Mailchimp Email Marketing Benchmarks study saw average click-through rates of 2.43%.[17]

Note: Your subject line sells the open while your email content sells the click. Don't confuse one for the other.

It's easy to get lulled into a false sense of security because some stats and metrics give an inflated sense of reality. What if you get a 50% open rate but no click-throughs to your sales pages or to your content?

If very few of your subscribers are taking action on your email content, consider the following:

- Is the email poorly written?

- Is the call to action clear?

- Was it badly timed (holidays, etc.)

- Is the email distracting?

- Are there too many topics in your email?

The same goes for engagement. Is it ok if subscribers throw heaps of engagement at you but never buy from you at all?

No, right?

So engagement is a good sign but don't let that lull you into a false sense of security.

Do they take action?

Do they click through on your emails?

Or do they just open them?

Are you increasingly getting more sales as your list grows?

Don't end up paying lip service to vanity metrics without knowing how they directly affect your business.

CLEAN YOUR LIST

Did you know that an email list decays by about 22.5% every year?[18]

If you have been growing your list for some time, you will need to clean your list, i.e., get rid of subscribers who have not opened or engaged with your emails in a three- to six-month period.

It's painful to delete those hard-earned subscribers, but it will be worth it because your open rates and engagement rates will increase. You will get a clearer picture of your stats as well as what your subscribers resonate with. You also don't want to keep paying for those unengaged subscribers on your list.

This is important because

1. The higher the number of inactive subscribers you have, the lower your engagement rates. For instance, if you email 10,000 people and only 1,500 recipients open your emails, your open rate is 15%. If 4,000 of those people are inactive and you decide to not email them, your open rate jumps to 25%. You get a better picture of your stats and what content as well as what email subject lines resonate more with your audience.

2. The lower your opens and clicks, the lower your **sender score or sender reputation**. Each of the email delivery providers gives you a sender score. The lower it is, the higher the chances of your emails being placed in the promotions or junk folder. This hurts the placement of your email in the inbox even for people who may be opening your emails.

While it's normal for your open rate to drop as your email list grows, it's still important to clean your list on a regular basis.

HOW TO CLEAN YOUR EMAIL LIST

Step 1: Identify cold subscribers

Does your email service provider help you maintain a cold subscriber list? If so, move on to Step 2. If it doesn't, create a segment of people who clicked and opened your emails over a three- to six-month period.

Step 2: Run a reengagement campaign

Tag these subscribers as "cold subscribers." Remove this segment from any of your ongoing email campaigns. You will immediately see an increase in your open and click-through rates.

Then craft a series of 2–3 emails letting this segment of subscribers know that they haven't opened or engaged with your emails and ask if they would still like to be on your list.

Give them the option to stay on your list and to indicate their interest by clicking on a link. You could also invite them to unsubscribe if the content doesn't serve them anymore. Remind them that anyone who doesn't click on the link will be unsubscribed. Once they click the link, remove the "cold subscriber" tag from them. You can delete anyone who doesn't click on your link within the period of time you've set (preferably within 5–7 days).

A reengagement campaign helps to determine the accuracy of your cold subscriber list. Depending on the email client that your subscribers are using (e.g., MacMail or Microsoft Outlook), some subscribers may be wrongly tagged as cold because their email opens are often not registered. You want to avoid the mistake where an engaged subscriber is deleted off your list.

It's not uncommon to have two thousand or more cold subscribers.

Sidekick removed a whopping thirty-eight thousand subscribers who were not engaging with their content.[19]

Image source[20]

ACTION

When did you last do a list clean? Pick a date and schedule your next list clean.

What type of emails get you the most engagement from your email list?

What type of subject lines get you the most opens from your email list?

TIPS TO WRITE EMAILS THAT GET CLICKS AND OPENS WRITE EMAILS FOR SKIMMERS

Long emails work fine especially if you enjoy writing them and your readers enjoy receiving them too. But long emails need to be made readable. You want to avoid "bricks" or huge paragraphs with long sentences.

Scroll through your inbox and you're bound to see an email like that. In cases like these, the reader never gets through the entire email, skims through most of it, or chucks it into a folder to read later.

What you can do:

Make the first sentence of your email attention-grabbing and short. Make it easy for your subscribers to move down the screen. People need to feel like they are actually making progress through your email. If they take one glance and see a huge block of text with no white space, they're going to flag your email, chuck it in a folder for later, or just forget about it.

Here are some rules you can follow to ensure that your emails are readable:

- Ensure each paragraph consists of three sentences maximum

- One point or thought = one sentence

- Bold important words to bring the reader's focus on them

- Use "you" in your emails so that your reader identifies with them

USE A POSTSCRIPT (P.S.)

An unused P.S. is wasted email real estate. Here are three ways you can use your P.S.

1. To remind them of the call to action in the email.

2. To build anticipation for your next email by placing an open loop. For example: Do you know what's the #1 mistake people make when it comes to meal planning? If you're thinking X, then you're wrong. I'll tell you what that mistake is next week and how it'll make you look at meal planning differently.

3. To get your subscribers thinking by raising questions in your emails. Rhetorical questions are a great way to engage your subscribers and get them to reply to you.

WRITE LIKE YOU TALK

Here's what a reader shared with me:

"I'm struggling to unlearn all the writing skills I acquired over the years in school. It's not easy to write in an easy, conversational manner."

Writing for the web is inherently different from the writing we're used to in school or college.

The same struggle carries over to email. But the more you practice, the better your conversational style of writing gets. Using ellipses, starting sentences with the words *or, and*, or *but*—these style choices are ok and make you look human. (I've used them several times throughout this book.)

START EMAILS BY DROPPING THE READER RIGHT IN THE MIDDLE OF THE ACTION

Remember in school when you used to write your introduction paragraph?

"It was a bright sunny morning…the flowers were…"

That's the warm-up text—the niceties before you get to the meat of the story.

But with email, you don't want to do that.

You want to plonk your reader right in the middle of the meat of your email—cut to the chase and pull the reader into the crux of the issue you're discussing in your email. This holds their attention, and they know clearly what you want them to do or get out of the email.

What you can do:
Go through your last few emails.

Read the first 3–5 sentences.

If you cut them out, would the reader still be able to understand your email—would it still retain its message? Then you know that you need to snip them out.

It might feel jarring…It might even make you feel uneasy to write in this way. It takes quite a bit of getting used to, but it brings your email alive with one simple tweak.

MAKE EMAIL SUBJECT LINES CLEAR, CATCHY, AND ACTIONABLE

Most subject lines fall under the following categories:

- Curiosity

- Urgency or scarcity

- Special offers

- Social proof (e.g., How I did…/THIS made me…)

- Benefit

- Story (e.g., I failed…/I never thought…)

Experiment with subject line styles from different categories. See what attracts your audience.

If your email service provider has an A/B or split test function, use it. Incorporate symbols or emojis to get attention as well. But don't overdo them or they lose their effect on your subscribers.

HAVE A CLEAR SIMPLE CALL TO ACTION

Check this out and then do this and then do that…

Ever received an email with several calls to action?

Avoid having too many calls to action unless your email style is that of a curated newsletter or roundup. But that doesn't mean you need to get stingy with your links. You should include more than one link in your emails. Ideally, you should include links in the top, middle, end, and P.S. of your emails. That's how many you can include. But don't drown your emails with several calls to action. If you do, your most important one gets buried and your subscribers never take action on what you want them to.

ACTION

Have a look at emails within your existing sequences and broadcasts and analyze them based on these questions:

Does your email tell them exactly what you want them to do?

Do all your emails have just one goal?

Have you included a P.S?

If you're including a link in your email, did you repeat it at least three times in the email?

TIPS TO CREATE EMAIL SYSTEMS

Systems are processes that you can set up once and then automate.

There are several features within email service providers that allow you to set up different systems with varying benefits for your business. But a quick warning that this very much depends on the capabilities of your email service provider. I've also used terms such as *tag*, *link trigger*, and *segment*, but these same features could go by a different term within your email service provider. In this section, we'll take a look at a few different systems you can set up.

USE EMAIL TO IDENTIFY POTENTIAL CUSTOMERS

Why does someone visit a sales page and not buy?

These are people who have shown an interest in your product because they bothered to click through. They may still have questions about your offer. They may need an extra nudge or some reassurance before they buy. Provide reassurance in a timely manner and you could very well bag that sale. We briefly spoke about how a retargeting ad can be used to send reminders about your offer to people who have already visited your sales page. But what if you don't have money to spend on ads? What if you could still identify potential customers and architect a return path to your sales page?

How to put this to work?

Identify anyone who's clicked on your sales page link in your email with a tag called "Prospect." You can then send them tailored email content where you call out that you're aware they've seen the sales page and invite them to ask questions or send them a midcart bonus. Once they purchase your product, set up an automation such that the "Prospect" tag is removed. This way, you can stop sending sales emails to people who have already bought your product.

USE EMAIL TO PROVIDE EXCELLENT CUSTOMER SERVICE ON AUTO

Your email content just bagged you a sale. That's fantastic, but your support for that subscriber who just purchased doesn't end there. Connect them to a new email sequence that handholds them through your course or product.

How to put this to work?

When someone purchases your product, tag them as "Purchased Product X" and then send out an automatic welcome email sequence for that product. You can also exclude subscribers who have this tag from receiving any further sales emails about this product.

GET MORE GRANULAR WITH AUDIENCE INTERESTS

Want to get even more granular with audience interests? Now you can!

You can use email to know *exactly* what your audience is interested in.

How to put this to work?

Tag anyone who has opted in to your freebie or content upgrade or clicked on a blog post link as interested in that particular topic. This way, when you're looking for beta testers for a product or to do a product survey related to the topic, you will know who to reach out to on your list.

USE EMAIL TO IDENTIFY YOUR CHEER-LEADERS

Who is opening and reading your emails?

Who is engaging with your emails and interacting with you?

Who has bought from you repeatedly?

These people are your cheerleaders.

If you nurture them well, they are highly likely to become your brand advocates.

Brand advocates spread the word about you and your brand. They tag you in Facebook groups. They tell their friends about you, refer clients your way, and spread your message. They help you grow your brand and in turn your business.

How to put this to work?
Some email service providers have a scoring system for each subscriber, allowing you to tell who your most engaged members are. Keep a system where you regularly identify these engaged subscribers. These are the subscribers most likely to provide a testimonial or review if you reach out to them.

USE EMAILS TO COLLECT TESTIMONI-ALS ON AUTO

Social proof is huge.

A recent survey by Collective Bias, an influencer agency, revealed that "30 percent of consumers are more likely to purchase a product endorsed by a non-celebrity blogger than a celebrity. Of that number, 70 percent of 18 to 34-year-olds had the highest preference for 'peer' endorsement."[21]

This means that your readers are looking for the opinions and experiences of someone like them. So by having testimonials of your own subscribers and readers on your blog, you're far more likely to come across as someone they can trust.

But do you struggle with asking your subscribers to give you a testimonial or asking them to share your work? There's no reason to feel uncomfortable with asking your subscribers for a testimonial or a favor if you have reason to believe that you've provided value every step of the way. If you think they are ready for that next stage to provide you with a testimonial, don't be afraid to ask.

How to put this to work?
Set up an automated email that goes out a set period of time (e.g., thirty days) after someone purchases your product or completes your welcome sequence and asks them for a testimonial. You could also autosend an email to any client after they've signed up for your service package and ask for feedback about the working process. This way you'll get your much-needed social proof and do it on auto. You will wake up each morning to testimonials in your inbox rather than have to actively look for them or remember to get in touch with subscribers, customers, or clients.

USE EMAIL TO UNDERSTAND THE AUDIENCE YOU'VE ATTRACTED

I'm a fan of the one-click survey — a simple question that allows you to tag subscribers based on their answers. Depending on how you structure your question, this could give you a lot of insight into the type of list you have and the stage your subscribers are at.

It's not a must but offering a free download for the click will incentivize them further.

How to put this to work?
- Decide on the choices you want in your survey.

- Then set up a simple trigger and tag for each of those options. You can then direct subscribers who click on it to a "Thank you for letting me know" page or a "Thank you and here's your free download" page.

NON-NEGOTIABLE TAGS AND SEGMENTS

The tags and segments you set up will be specific to your business. But there are some that are plain good practice. (**Note:** X = topic/product.)

- Purchased product X (exclude these subscribers from promotions)

- Interested in X (based on opt-in or email clicks)

- Downloaded specific content upgrade/opt-in X

- In email sequence X (exclude these subscribers from your broadcast emails and promotions)

FAQ 14: What exactly is segmentation and how do I use it?

A segment is a group of subscribers who

a. fulfill certain conditions that you have set or

b. take certain actions

The purpose of segmentation is to avoid list exhaustion where you send too many emails or send emails that are irrelevant to your subscribers. By segmenting your list, you're able to tailor your content to different groups of subscribers. You can use what members of a segment have in common to deliver more relevant emails to that segment.

Here are two ways you can segment your audience:

1. Behavior based on actions taken in emails – You create a segment of subscribers who

have clicked on links related to a specific topic in your emails or clicked to sign up for specific events in an email.

2. Entry point – You create a segment based on what they opted in to.

ACTION

Which of these systems are you missing? Make a list of systems you can set up today.

CONCLUSION +
NEXT STEPS

You now have more than a bare-bones framework to put in place an email marketing strategy for your business.

Rather than flit from week to week wondering what to write about and winging it, imagine creating an email strategy that enables you to take the weekend off and still see your list grow, rake in testimonials, and make sales.

Imagine having endless content ideas...

Imagine creating an opt-in offer with all the right ingredients that has readers clamoring to get their hands on it...

Imagine sending emails with confidence knowing exactly the impact that particular email will have on your subscribers...

That's the power of an email marketing strategy!

But it's easy to get sucked into an endless cycle of planning rather than "shipping." You can conceptualize and plan for an endless number of sequences and lead magnets without finishing any of them. That's one of the biggest struggles I see with my clients and students.

You can't have every single automation or system I've outlined in the book from the start. You can't have multiple sequences set up all at once for each of your lead magnets if you've never created a sequence before. Take incremental steps every single day.

As your list grows over time and as you build your brand and stake claim to your expertise, you will attract more people who go on to buy from you. But it's important to remember that email is not a medium you use only to sell.

Email is also a content marketing tool you use to be top of mind and build trust with your audience. You can read several books, blogs, and emails that say you have to be consistent with email marketing. But if you don't believe in it, it'll never become a part of your business and content marketing strategy.

Turning subscribers into brand advocates takes time.

You have to stand out in that busy inbox.

You have to fight to get noticed.

You have to show them you care.

You have to earn their trust.

But it's well worth the effort because you are nurturing your own marketing team—people who will show up for your brand when you need them to.

I hope you give your business a simple email marketing strategy and a chance to build an audience that's addicted to your zone of genius.

Before you go, remember to download your bonuses at https://meera.email/300 and sign up for the FREE Email Crash Course at https://meera.email/challenge.

Good luck and thank you for sharing your work with the world!

THANK YOU FOR READING

I hope you enjoyed reading this book.

I really appreciate your feedback, and I love hearing what you have to say.

Could you leave me a review on Amazon letting me know what you thought of the book?

Thank you so much! If you want to get in touch, come find me here at my slice of the internet: https://www.meerakothand.com.

Meera

About the Author

Meera is an email marketing strategist and 3X Amazon best-selling author of the books *The One Hour Content Plan*, *But I'm not an Expert & Your First 100*. She is also the publisher of **MeeraKothand.Com**, an award-winning site listed as one of the 100 Best Sites for Solopreneurs in 2017 and 2018, and the popular CREATE Planners. Using her unique Profitable Email System™ and ADDictive Business Framework, she makes powerful marketing strategies simple and relatable so that small business owners can build a tribe that's addicted to their zone of genius.

Other Books on Amazon

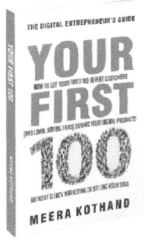

RESOURCES

1. Marco Mijatovic, "4 Compelling Stats that Prove email Marketing is Alive," Mailjet, June 29, 2017, https://www.mailjet.com/blog/news/stats-email-marketing/.

2. Matthew Collis, "Why you shouldn't underestimate email marketing: statistics," The American Genius, November 14, 2012, https://theamericangenius.com/business-marketing/why-you-shouldnt-underestimate-the-value-of-email-marketing/.

3. Casey Hampsey, "Saturday Stat Series: The Influence of Email Marketing Messages," Data & Marketing Association, August 3, 2013, https://thedma.org/blog/data-driven-marketing/saturday-stat-series/.

4. Jeremy Miller, *Sticky Branding: 12.5 Principles to Stand Out, Attract Customers, and Grow an Incredible Brand* (Toronto; Dundurn Press, 2015) https://www.amazon.com/dp/1459728106/.

5. Matt Rosoff, "People either check email all the time, or barely at all," Business Insider, August 17, 2015, https://www.businessinsider.com/how-often-do-people-check-their-email-2015-8/?IR=T.

6. "Make Money With Email Even If You Have a Small List," *Baer on Marketing*, https://baeronmarketing.com/make-money-with-email-even-if-you-have-a-small-list/.

7. Julie Verhulst and Kristina Epping, "First Impressions Email Marketing Study," Ciceron, March 2013, https://www.slideshare.net/CiceronHQ/first-impressions-email-study-22872415/.

8. "Why I Invested in ConvertKit vs Mailchimp When I Was Earning $0 from My Blog," *Meera Kothand*, https://www.meerakothand.com/convert-kit-vs-mailchimp/.

9. "15 Email Marketing Myths," Email Monks, https://emailmonks.com/mythbusting/15-email-marketing-myths-infographic.html.

10. Sançar Sahin, "Why do people unsubscribe from email newsletters?" GetApp Lab, March 3, 2015, https://lab.getapp.com/new-research-getdata-why-do-people-unsubscribe-from-email-newsletters/.

11.Eyrn Branham, Text-based vs Image-based Emails – Which One Does Better?" Pinpointe, September 8, 2017, https://www.pinpointe.com/blog/text-based-vs-image-based-emails-which-does-better.

12. Bettina Specht, "The 2017 Email Client Market Share [Infographic]," Litmus, January 25, 2018, https://litmus.com/blog/the-2017-email-client-market-share-infographic.

13. Emil Kristensen, "Here's Why Emails Go to Spam (and What to Do About It)," Sleeknote, March 21, 2018, https://sleeknote.com/blog/why-emails-go-to-spam.

14. Welcome Messages Get Highest Open Rates of All Email Campaigns: How to Improve Yours, MarketingSherpa, December 9, 2004, https://www.

marketingsherpa.com/article/how-to/how-to-improve-yours.

15. McKenzie Gregory, "9 welcome emails that had us at 'hello,'"Emma, May 10, 2016, https://content.myemma.com/blog/9-welcome-emails-that-had-us-at-hello-2.

16. Emma Brudner, "Email Open Rates By Industry: See How You Stack Up," HubSpot, October 15, 2018, https://blog.hubspot.com/sales/average-email-open-rate-benchmark.

17. "Email Marketing Benchmarks," Mailchimp, https://mailchimp.com/resources/email-marketing-benchmarks/.

18. "How Inbound Marketing Helps Overcome Database Decay," HubSpot, https://www.hubspot.com/database-decay.

19. "Applying a Product Mindset to Content", Anum Hussain, http://www.anumhussain.com/presentations/product-growth-mindset-content.

20. Katie Lantukh, "9 Effective Email Unsubscribe Pages," HubSpot, February 2, 2015, https://blog.hubspot.com/marketing/email-unsubscribe-pages.

21. Colleen Vaughan, "Do Celebrity Endorsements Still Matter for Marketing?" March 29, 2016,

https://www.collectivebias.com/blog/blog-2016-03-non-celebrity-influencers-drive-store-purchases.

Made in the USA
Monee, IL
14 January 2021